T0197626

Our Structure
of
Living Holy

DUANE PHILLIP CAREY JR.

Copyright © 2021 by Duane Phillip Carey Jr.. 835265

All rights reserved. No part of this book may
be reproduced or transmitted in any form or by
any means, electronic or mechanical, including
photocopying, recording, or by any information
storage and retrieval system, without permission
in writing from the copyright owner.

To order additional copies of this book, contact:
Xlibris
844-714-8691
www.Xlibris.com
Orders@Xlibris.com

Scripture taken from the King James Version of
the Bible.

ISBN: 978-1-6641-0949-0 (sc)
ISBN: 978-1-6641-0948-3 (e)

Print information available on the last page

Rev. date: 09/29/2021

Our Structure Of Living Holy

Administrative Office Of Trusting God's Instruction

Trials and tribulations are on every side in life today. Crime is becoming a natural for everyday living as God allows us to live to see another day. We have lost our focus on our creator, our Lord, and Saviour. We were formed within Jesus likeness, and image, and we were created to live Holy, and set apart unto Christ. We were instructed in (Rom 12:2) Be not conformed to this world, but be ye transformed by the renewing of your mind, that ye may prove what is that good, and acceptable, and perfect will of God. We have to have the attitude to follow Christ, and continue to live right. Keep living don't give up (Phil 1:11) Being filled with the fruits of righteousness, which are led by Jesus Christ unto the glory, and praise of God.

Keep living don›t give up (Deut 31:8) And the Lord, He it is that doth go before thee, He will be with thee, neither forsake thee: fear not neither be dismayed. We have to just trust God, and remain open minded to remain connected to His word. (2 Cor 5:17) Therefore if any man be in Christ, he is a new creature: old things are passed away; behold all things are become new. Don't worry about the snares of this world, (Pro 3:5-6) Trust in the Lord with all thine heart; and lean not unto thine own understanding. In all thy ways acknowledge him, and He shall direct thy paths. Let us come together as a united nation in Christ. Sin is anything that does not glorify our Lord.

(Rom 6:23) For the wages of sin is death, but the gift of God is eternal life in Christ Jesus our Lord. The choice is yours will you receive the Lord for your salvation for the remission of sins so that you can be imparted within the Holy path of life.

Our structure, and character in life enlightens our mindset on how we should utilize our living advances. Once we are able to sustain our differences, and come together as one. We have to stand on one accord, and empower one another with encouragement. We are challenged to strive to make the best of our success in life. We have to always remember to always put God first place in life. Without you Lord we are lost on every side, and our goals are neglected because we have not made the decision to live righteously. Now that our focus is clear Jesus prepared our table of life unto righteousness. Our living arrangements have been sustained within the image of Christ. (Ps 55:22) Cast all your cares on the Lord, and he will sustain you; He shall never suffer the righteous to be moved. Our motivation is clear, and our mindset is identified with the direction of our Lord, and Saviour Jesus who's over all. Let's give Jesus all the honor, glory, and praise as He secures our hearts, and minds from harm's way.

As we proceed to our next our structure in Christ is to consecrate our hearts to be set aside, and dedicated for God›s use. (Lev 20:7) (Sanctify yourselves therefore, and be ye Holy for I am the Lord your God

(Rom 8:29) For whom he did foreknow, he also did predestinate to be conformed to the image of his Son that he might be the first born among many brethren. Our conversion is to become mediators of Christ. One who makes peace between two people or two groups who are not displeased or angry with one another. Life is God's purpose, and the plan for everlasting life was originated through His love toward all creation. It's a matter of time before the restoration process would be enlightened to take part within our souls. Ps 119:9 Wherewithal shall a young man cleanse his way? By taking heed thereto according to thy word. (Pro 1:5) A wise man will hear, and increase learning, and a man of understanding shall attain unto wise counsels.

Life is beautiful as we begin to open our hearts, and minds to accept what›s been given, and acceptable to Christ. Our way of thinking should line up with the word of God so that as we grow the enlightenment, and contentment of our joy would last forevermore. My heart is overjoyed because when I think of

all that God has done in my life, and all that He›s doing at this present time my soul cries out Hallelujah. As we come together to understand the acknowledgement of Christ we are bound to accept what is true. Jesus› love for us was so dedicated for our lives that we were acquitted free from punishment or blame throughout our sinful nature. Our affliction of being exposed to sin that leads to trouble or pain discourages our mindset deeply. (Rom 3:25) Whom God hath set forth to be the propitiation through faith in his blood to declare his righteousness for the remission of sins that our past through the forbearance of God. Our payment that convicts the relationship between God, and his children is that He gave his all so that we could be free.

Throughout our faith within Jesus Christ is accessible to all that believe.

(Rom 3:22) Even the righteousness of God which is by faith of Jesus Christ unto all, and upon all them that believe: for there is no difference. (Jn 14:6) Jesus said I am the way, the truth, and the life no man cometh to the Father, but by me. We are blessed because of our belief in God for holiness is to all that believe. (Eph 5:30) For we are members of his body. The body is a unit though it is made up. (Rom 12:14) Bless them which persecute you: bless, and curse not. (Rom 12:16) Be of the same mind one toward another. Mind not high things, but condescend to men of low estate. Be not wise in your own conceits. It's an honor, and a privilege being called by God to maintain a position of righteousness. (Phil 1:6) Being confident of this very thing that He which hath begun a good work in you will perform it until the day of Jesus Christ:

(Pro 14:25) (A true witness delivereth souls: but the deceitful speaketh lies.

(Pro 14:16 A wise man feareth, and is confident.

As we come together to receive God›s direction, and enlightenment.

(Pro 1:2) To know wisdom, and instruction is to perceive the words of understanding. (Pro 1:8) My son hear the instruction of thy father, and forsake not the law of thy mother. (Pro 1:9) For they shall be an ornament of grace unto thy head, and chains around thy neck. (Ps 119:130) The entrance of thy

words giveth light it giveth understanding to the simple. Our understanding in Christ is wisdom, and knowledge: (Pro 2:2) So that thou incline thy ear unto wisdom, and apply thine heart unto understanding. (Pro 2:6 For the Lord giveth wisdom;

out of his mouth cometh knowledge, and understanding. There isn't anything too hard for God. (Jer 32:27) Behold I am the Lord thy God of all flesh. Is there anything too hard for me? There is power in the name: (Jer 10:6) For as much as there is none like unto thee O Lord thou art great, and thy name is great in might.

It was the power of his divine message: (Lu 4:32) And they were astonished at his doctrine for the word was with power. God›s divine power relinquished: (Lu 14:14) And thou shalt be blessed for they cannot recompense thee for thou shalt be recompensed at the resurrection of the just. We are ordained by God to maintain witnessing power: (Acts 1:8) But ye shall receive power after that Holy Ghost is come you, and ye shall be witness unto me both in Jerusalem, and in all Judea, and in Samaria, and unto the uttermost parts of the earth. Being called by God to be transformed, inspired, empowered, enlightened, and motivates our hearts for Holy living. God has, and always will be our provider, sustainer, healer, comforter, and way maker no matter what trials of tribulations that we may go through. It›s important that we seek God first with all our hearts so that the contentment of our joy can be edified forevermore.

Let us come together, and love one another, and encourage each other so that as we have been transformed in the likeness, and image of Christ our hearts can be settled, and guaranteed to live righteously for God. (Ps 18:2)

The Lord is my rock, and my fortress, and my deliverer, my God, my strength in whom I will trust my shield, and my horn of my salvation my stronghold.

(Ps 71:2) Deliver me in your righteousness, and cause me to escape: incline thine ear unto me, and save me. (Ps 90:1) Lord thou hast been thy dwelling place in all generations. (Pro 3:5-6) Trust in the Lord with all thine heart, and lean not unto thine own understanding. 6 In all thy ways acknowledge him, and He shall direct thy paths. (Rom 4:12) Having the ability, and direction from the most high God enlightens my heart, mind, and soul to win the race.

I am very proud, and excited to be used by God to accomplish true success. The instruction of scripture makes it clear to understand that once we are led by God's laws we are equipped for success. Our standards of understanding the accountability of our actions is first of all acknowledging the biblical principles that each person is answerable to God, and responsible for its actions. God's word is motivation, and direction of living a successful spirit filled lifestyle. Our goal is to come together as a body of Christ. I pray that throughout God's expression of scripture, faith, and encouragement would enlighten our hearts, minds, and souls. Let's be positioned with the helmet of faith as we live our lives in Christ. (Ps 19:4) Let the words of my mouth, and the meditation of my heart be found acceptable in thy sight, O Lord, my rock, and my redeemer.

Administrative Office
Of Holy Living

Walking within the progression of the Lord our identity is to imitate

Jesus' likeness, and image. We were created to live Holy unto God with all manner of life. (2 Cor 5:17) Therefore if any man be in Christ, he is a new creature: old things are passed away, behold, all things become new. (Ps 36:9) For with thee is the fountain of life; in thy light we shall see light. (Ps 37:5) Commit thy way unto the Lord trust also in him, and He shall bring it to pass. (Ps 37:4 Delight thyself also in the Lord, and He will give thee the desires of your heart. Our motivation in Christ as we walk in the new realm of creation.

We are instructed in (Mk 12:30) And thou shalt love the Lord thy God with all thy heart, and with all thy soul, and with all thy mind, and with all thy strength this is the first commandment. (Col 3:16) Let the word of Christ dwell in you richly in all wisdom teaching, and admonishing one another in Psalms, hymns, and spiritual songs singing with grace in your hearts to the Lord.

(Phil 3:16) Nevertheless whereto we have already attained let us walk with the same rule let us mind the same thing. We are grateful to abide by God's mercy, and grace. (Tit 2:11) For the grace of God that bringeth salvation appeared to all men. 12 Teaching us that denying ungodliness, and worldly lust, we should live soberly, righteously, and godly in this present world. 13 Looking for that blessed hope, and the glorious opening of the great God, and Savior Jesus Christ. (1 Pet 1:3) Blessed be the God of our Father, and Lord Jesus Christ, which according to his abundant mercy hath begotten us again unto a lively hope by the resurrection of Jesus Christ from the dead.

As we seek God to live according to His purpose, and plan.

(Pro 8:8) All the words of my mouth are in righteousness there is nothing froward or perverse in them. (Pro 8:9) They are all plain to him that understandeth, and right to them that find knowledge. (Pro 8:10) (Receive my instruction, and not silver; and knowledge rather than choice gold. (Pro 19:2)

Also that the soul be without knowledge it is not good; and he that hasteth with his feet sinneth. (Pro 24:14) So shall the knowledge of wisdom be unto thy soul then thou hast found it, then there shall be a reward, and thy expectation shall not be cut off. (Pro 8:7) For my mouth shall speak truth; and wickedness is an abomination to my lips. Once we make our decision to follow God's direction

(Phil 4:7) And the peace of God which passeth all understanding shall keep your hearts, and minds through Christ Jesus. Our mindset is to retain God's leadership that gives us the substance of knowledge. (Pro 24:5) A wise man is strong: yea a man of knowledge increaseth strength. (Pro 2:3) Yea if thou criest after knowledge, and liftest up thy voice for understanding. Our understanding concerning God's instruction would be more clearer to acknowledge, and understand righteous living.

As we are led by God throughout receiving direction from his Holy Word we have a better understanding of how we were directed to live. (Pro 1:5)

A wise will hear, and increase learning, and a man of understanding shall attain unto wise counsels. (Pro 1:6) To understand a proverb, and the interpretation of the wise, and their dark sayings. Once we are secure with the enlightenment of who we are, we understand who we were created to be, our mindset has a better understanding. (Eph 1:17-18) That the God of our Lord Jesus Christ the Father of Glory may give unto you the Spirit of wisdom, and revelation in the knowledge of him. 18. The eyes of your understanding being enlightened: that ye may know what is the hope of his calling, and what the riches of the glory of his inheritance in his saints.

Administration Office
Of Understanding

It's important to have a clear understanding of God's instruction in life to maintain a prosperous mindset that produces successful living. (Pro 15:14)

The heart of him that hath understanding seeketh knowledge; but the mouth of the fools feedeth on foolishness. (Pro 10:13) In the lips of him that hath understanding wisdom is found: but a rod is for the back of him that is void of understanding. (Pro 14:18) The simple inherit folly; but the prudent are crowned with knowledge. Prudent: Wise in practical matters, Careful for one's interest provident, Careful about one's circumspect. (1 Jn 3:9) Whosoever is born of God doth not sin: for his seed remaineth in him: and he cannot sin because he is born of God. (1 Jn 3:11) For this is the message that ye heard from the beginning: that we should love one another. (Rom 12:2) And be not conformed to this world: but be ye transformed by the renewing of your mind that ye may prove what is that good, and acceptable, and perfect will of God.

Administrative Office
Of The Heart

We have to have an open heart for God to receive the acknowledgement of God›s Holy Word. We were not directed to harden our hearts unto God because there are consequences behind it. (Zach 7:12) Yeah they made their hearts as an adamant stone lest they should hear the law, and the words which the Lord of host hath sent in his Spirit by the former prophets therefore came a great wrath from the Lord of host. God knows our inner hearts: (Sam 16:7) But the Lord looked unto Samuel Look not on his countenance; or the height of his stature; because I refused him; for the Lord seeth not as a man seeth; for a man looketh on the outward appearance, but the Lord looketh on the heart. (Job 23:16) For God maketh my heart soft, and the Almighty troubled me.

As we are led by God we understand that He›s the center of our emotions. (Ps 26: 2-3) Examine me O Lord, and prove me, try my reins, and my heart. 3. For thy loving kindness is before mine eyes; and I have walked in truth. (Ps 51:10) Create in me a clean heart, O God, and renew a right spirit in me. (Ps 51:2-3) Wash me throughly from mine iniquity, and cleanse me from my sin. 3 For I acknowledge my transgression, and my sin is ever before me.

(Ps 38:10) My heart panteth my strength faileth me, as for the light of mine eyes it also is gone from me. (Ecc 3:11) He hath made everything beautiful in his time also He hath set the world in their heart so that no man can find out the work that God maketh from the beginning to the end.

Administrative Office
Of The Mind

It›s important to have an open mindset for Christ because

(Ps 91:11) The Lord knoweth the thoughts of a man, that they are vanity.

It's important to focus on having a heart for God because the forces of evil are in the midst. (Jer 4:14) O Jerusalem, wash thine heart from wickedness that thou mayest be saved, How long shall the vain thoughts lodge within thee?

As men, and women of God we are directed not to have depraved mindsets.

(Rom 1:28) And even as they did not like to retain God in their knowledge,

God gave them over to a reprobate mind to do those things which are not convenient. Oftentimes we find ourselves dealing with conflict between our mind, and body. (Rom 7:21) I find then a law that, when I would do good, evil is present with me.

It›s not God›s desire for us to be controlled by our natural mind, but by the Spirit mindset of Christ. (Rom 8:6-9) For to be carnally minded is death:

but to be Spiritually minded is life, and peace. 7 Because the carnal mind is enmity against God; for it is not subject to the law of God, neither indeed can be. 8. So then they that are in the flesh cannot please God. 9.But ye are not in the flesh, but in the Spirit, if so be that the Spirit of God dwell in you. Now if any man have not the Spirit of Christ, he is none of his.

Our attitudes of our mind dictates conduct: (Phil 4:8-9) (Finally brethren, whatsoever things are true, whatsoever things are honest, whatsoever things are just, whatsoever things are pure, whatsoever things are lovely, whatsoever things are of a good report; if there be any virtue, and there be praise think on these things. 9. Those things which ye have both learned, and received, and heard, and seen in me, do: and the God of peace shall be with you. We are not instructed by God to have a corrupt mindset; (Tit 1:15) Unto the pure all things are pure, but unto them that are defiled, and unbelieving is nothing is pure; but even their mind, and conscience is defiled.

We are led by God to maintain our thought process fixed on Jesus;

(Heb 3:1) Wherefore holy brethren partakers of the heavenly callin, consider the Apostle, and the High Priest of our profession Christ Jesus. Within our christian lifestyle prepares our mindset for action, (1 Pet 1:13) Wherefore gird up your loins of your mind, be sober, and hope to the end of your grace that is to be brought unto you at the revelation of Jesus Christ.

Administrative Office Of The Soul

Our souls belongs to God we were created by God alone, (Gen 2:7) And the Lord God formed man of the dust of the ground, and breathe air into his nostrils the breath of life, and man became a living soul. Once God return for us our bodies will remain on earth, but our Spirit will return to God. (Ecc 12:7) Then shall the dust return to the earth as it was: and the Spirit shall return to God who gave it. We were instructed by God to love Him with all thine heart, and with all thy soul, and with all thy might. We belong to God our creator,

(Eze 18:4) Behold all souls are mine, and the soul of thy Father, so also the soul of the Son is mine, the soul that sinneth shall die.

It›s very important to acknowledge, and serve God with all your heart, mind, and soul, and body because the devil is on every side seeking whom he may tear down. We are safe because God paid the price in full. (Mt 16:26) For what is a man profited if he shall gain the whole world, and lose his own soul? or what shall a man give in exchange for his soul? (Mt 10:28) And fear not them which kill the body, but are not able to destroy both soul, and body. (Acts 2:27) Because thou will not leave my soul in hell neither wilt thou suffer thine Holy One to see corruption. We have to recognize that God is in control.

(Ps 23: 1-5 The Lord is my Shepherd: I shall not want. 2 He maketh me lie down in green pastures: He leadeth me beside the still waters, 3 He restoreth my soul: He leadeth me in the path of righteousness for his name sake. 4. Yea though I walk through the shadow of death, I will fear no evil: for thou art with me; thy rod,and thy staff comfort me. 5. Thou preparest a table before me in the presence of mine enemies; thou anointed my head with oil; my cup runneth over. Surely goodness, and mercy shall follow me all the day of my life; and I will dwell in the house of the Lord forever. Amen

We cannot remain living within our sinful nature: (Eze 18:20) The soul that sinneth, it shall die. The son shall not bear the iniquity of the father, neither shall the father bear iniquity of the son: the righteousness of the righteous shall be upon him, and the wickedness of the wicked shall be upon him.

(1Cor 15:51) Behold I shew you a mystery: we shall not sleep, but we shall all be changed. (Acts 2:1) Then they that gladly receive his word were baptized, and the same day they were added unto them about three thousand souls.

Administrative Office Of The Body

Our bodies were created, redeemed for the use of Jesus Christ our Lord, and Saviour; (Job 19:25) (For I know that my redeemer liveth, and that He shall stand at the latter day of the earth: 26. And thou after my skin worms destroy this body, yet in my flesh shall I see God: (Job 21:23) One dieth in his full strength, being wholly at ease, and quiet. 24. His breasts are full of milk, and his bones are moistened with marrow. 25. And another dieth in the bitterness of his soul, and never eateth with pleasure. 26. They shall lie down alike in the dust, and the worms shall cover them.

We were given the power to cast out devils, and their demonic power over our lives. (Mt 8:31-32) (So the devil besought him saying If thou cast us out suffer us to go away in the herd of the swine, 32 and He said unto them, Go. and when they were come out they went into the herd of the swine: and behold the whole herd of swine ran violently down a steep place into the sea, and perished in the waters. (Rom 6:19) I speak after the manner of men because of the infirmity of your flesh; for as ye have yielded your members servants to righteousness unto holiness. (1Cor 3:16-17) (Know ye not that ye are the temple of God, and that the spirit of God dwelleth in you? 17. If any man defile the temple of God, him shall God destroy; for the temple of God is Holy, which temple ye are.

Administrative Office
Of Sanctification

We were blessed to be led by God to live, and walk within the ram of holiness throughout our sanctification in Christ. (1 Cor 6:11) And such were some of you: but ye are washed, but ye are sanctified, but ye are justified in the name of the Lord Jesus, and by the Spirit of our God. (1 Pet 3:15) But sanctify the Lord in your heart, and always be ready to give an answer to every man that asketh you a reason of the hope that is in you with meekness, and fear. (Acts 1:12) Neither is there salvation in any other for there is none other name under heaven given among men where we must be saved. (Jn 3:10) In this the children of God are manifest, and the children of the devil: whosoever doth not righteousness is not of God, neither he that loveth not his brother.

(Pro 18:1) Through desire a man having separated himself seeketh intermeddleth with all wisdom. 2. A fool hath no delight in understanding, but his heart may discover itself.

Administrative Office
Of Restoration

(Pro 15:9) Be angry, and sin not : let not the sun go down upon your wrath:

(Heb 12:1) Wherefore seeing we also are compassed about with a great cloud of witness, let us lay aside every weight, and the sin which doth so easily beset us, and let us run with patience the race that is before us.

(1 Jn 3:4) Whosoever committeth sin transgresseth also the law: for sin is the transgression of the law. (1 Jn 3:8) He that committeth sin is of the devil; for the devil sinneth from the beginning. For this purpose the Son of God was manifested that he might destroy the works of the devil. (1 Cor 5:7) Purge out therefore the old that ye may be a new lump as you were unleavened. For even Christ our passover is sacrificed for us.

Administrative Office Of Unrighteous Living

(Pro 15:9) The way of the wicked is an abomination unto the Lord; but He loveth him that followeth after righteousness. (1Thess 5:22) Abstain from all appearance of evil. (Pro 18:18) (The lot causeth contentions to cease, and parteth between the mighty. (Jn 8:43-44) Why do you understand my speech? even because you cannot hear my word. 44 Ye are of your father the devil, and the lust of your father the devil ye will do. He is a murderer from the beginning, and abode not in the truth, because there is no truth in him. When he speaketh a lie, he speaketh of his own: for he is a liar, and the father of it. (Jn 16:19) Now Jesus knew that they were desirous to ask him, and said unto them, do you acquire among yourselves of that I said a little while, and ye shall not see me: and again, a little while.

Administrative Office Of Wisdom

(Ps 46:10) Be still, and know that I am God I will be exalted among the brethren,

I will be exalted in all the earth. (Ps 119:125) I am thy servant; give me understanding that I may know thy testimonies. (Pro 7:4) Say unto wisdom, thou are my sister; and call understanding thy kinswoman: (Isa 55:5) Behold thou shalt call nation that thou knowest not; and nations that knew not thee shall run unto because of the Lord thy God, and for the Holy one of Israel for he hath glorified thee. (Pro 24:5) A wise man is strong, yea a man of knowledge increaseth strength. (Jn 14:21) He that hath my commandments, and keep them he it is that loveth me shall be loved of my Father, and I will love him, and make our abode with him.

Administrative Office Of Cleansing The Body

(1 Cor 6:11) And such were some of you: but ye were washed, but ye are sanctified, but ye are justified in the name of the Lord Jesus.

(Pro 1:15) My son walk not thou in the way with them refrain thy foot from their path. (Rom 12:1-3) I beseech you therefore brethren by the mercies of God that ye present your bodies a living sacrifice Holy acceptable unto God which is your reasonable service. (Pro 18:4) The words of a mans mouth are as deep waters, and a wellspring of wisdom as a flowing brook. (Pro 16:23) The heart of the wise teached his mouth, and addeth learning to his lips. (Pro 8:13) The fear of the Lord is to hate evil, pride, arrogancy, and the evil way, and the froward do I hate. (Eph 4:26) Be ye angry, and sin not, let not the sun go down upon your wrath. (Pro 15:9) The way of the wicked is an abomination unto the Lord, but he that loveth him that followeth after righteousness. (1Pet 3:15) But sanctify the Lord in your hearts, and be ready always to give an answer to every man that asketh you a reason of the hope that is in you with meekness, and fear.

Administrative Office Of Direction

Wisdom: Knowledge grounded by insight, and understanding reverence for God is the source of wisdom.

(Lu 9:10) The fear of the Lord is the beginning of wisdom, and the knowledge of the Holy is understanding.

Knowledge: A body of facts or information gained through study, and experiences.

(Job: 36:12) But if they obey not they shall perish by the sword, and they shall die without knowledge.

Understanding: The quality of discernment comprehension, 2. The faculty by which one understands.

(Pro: 1:5) A wise man will hear, and increase learning, and a man of understanding shall attain unto wise counsels.

Structure: Something made up of parts that we put together in a particular way.

(Heb 3:4) For we are partakers of Christ if we hold the beginning of our confidence stedfast until the end.

Image: An exact likeness or representation of some object of idolatrous worship.

(Ex 34:34) For thou shalt worship no other God for the Lord whose name is zealous is a zealous God.

Holiness: Moral purity: To be set apart, and sanctified for service to God.

(Ex 15:11) Who is like unto thee, O Lord among the God's? who is like thee, glorious in holiness fearful in praises doing wonders.

Holy Spirit: Jesus promised He would send the Holy Spirit as a comforter, and advocate in his absence.

(Jn 14:16) And I will pray to the Father, and He will give you another comforter that He may abide with you forever.

Advocate: One who plead the cause of another.

(1 Jn 2:1) My little children these things I write unto you that ye sin not. And if a man sin we have an advocate with the Father Jesus Christ the righteous.

Inspiration: Divine influence God's inspiration as the source of human understanding.

(Job 32:8) But there is a good Spirit in man, and the inspiration of the Almighty giveth them understanding.

Image Of God: Human beings were created to perfectly reflect God's image married that image by sinning, but have the potential to be molded back into that image.

(Rom 8:28-30) And we know that all things work together for good to them that love God to them who are called according to his purpose.

Printed in the United States
by Baker & Taylor Publisher Services

Printed in the United States
by Baker & Taylor Publisher Services